CONTENTS

THE STORY OF A FAMILY

A family's story cannot be told in a paragraph or a page. It is marvelously complex, told by many narrators over many years, and is a tale of great love and great loss, filled with surprising twists and unforgettable characters. A family's story is a never-ending narrative. The tale continues, decade after decade. With each generation, new chapters are added to the story.

The story of a family is life-shaping. Whether you know it or not, your family's history has impacted your life journey in monumental ways. The experiences of your elders have helped form who you are and how you see the world. Their triumphs and tragedies act as a prologue to your life story.

Surprisingly, we often know very little about the journeys and inner lives of the people closest to us. Consider for a moment your grandparents. How much do you really know about them? Do you know how they met or when they were married? Do you know their favorite hobbies or early ambitions? Do you know their middle names? Often, our knowledge of family is more limited than we might think. In the hustle and bustle of the present moment, we forget to share our most important memories and stories with the ones we love.

Unfortunately, if the stories of your family aren't shared, they are lost in the passage of time. The purpose of this journal is to capture, preserve, and celebrate the stories of your family. Fill these pages with the most treasured stories of your nearest and dearest, from wild adventures in distant lands to special moments at home.

As you read their stories, your understanding of your family and how their lives have shaped your own will deepen. You may even begin to see generational patterns. Perhaps you and another family member share a common passion that you had been previously unaware of. Or, you might learn about a pivotal moment that helped shape your life and the lives of other family members.

HOW TO USE THIS JOURNAL

This book is comprised of six chapters. Each chapter focuses on different members of your family. In the first chapter, you will reflect on your own journey, answering prompts related to your childhood, teenage years, and adulthood. In the following chapters, you'll record tidbits and tales about your other family members. You will find that there are chapters dedicated to your parents, siblings, grandparents, cousins, and aunts and uncles.

Each chapter in this book contains thoughtful prompts, and each prompt is provided with ample space for response. This will allow for multiple family members' stories. It is ok if you don't know the answers yourself, so encourage family members to share as much as they can about their life journeys.

The light icons designate one side of your family and the dark icons the other:

Let them know that their stories are immensely important to you and that every detail they provide will be cherished.

Use this journal to learn where your family has been, how their journeys have shaped your own, and where they are heading in the future. A family's story is never finished. How will your family write its next chapter?

My Story

"To be yourself in a world that is constantly trying to make you something else is the greatest accomplishment."

—RALPH WALDO EMERSON

What is my earliest memory?

Where do I see myself in 10 years?

What are some of my favorite memories from elementary school?

Who were my first crushes? What do I remember about them?

Who were my best friends growing up? How were they different from each other?

Which parent was I closest to as a child? Has that changed?

How would I describe my high school self?

Who was my first love? Describe the relationship in as much detail as possible.

If I could change one thing about my teenage years, what would it be? Why?

What did I think was important in college? Has that changed?

What is one of my favorite memories from college?

How would I describe my style? How has it changed over the years?

What was one of the greatest challenges of my young adulthood?

What do I think are my best qualities?

What do I think I need to work on?

_____

_____

_____

_____

_____

_____

_____

_____

_____

_____

_____

_____

_____

_____

_____

_____

_____

_____

_____

_____

How have my values changed since I was young?

What is an activity I used to do all the time with my friends?

If I could relive one day, what would it be?

Do I consider myself a spiritual person? Why or why not?

What books, movies, and other works of art are important to me?

If I could live anywhere, where would it be? Why?

What are three events that have shaped my life?

What are my favorite parts of life right now?

What would be my ideal retirement scenario?

My Dream Jobs

CHILDHOOD DREAM JOB	WHY THIS JOB SEEMED AWESOME	HOW I FEEL ABOUT THIS JOB NOW

Fill in each of these tables with as many dream jobs as you can remember and/or think of.

DREAM JOB NOW	WHY THIS JOB SEEMS AWESOME	HOW WOULD I GET THIS JOB?

My Top 10 Super-Secret Crushes

	NAME	REASON
1.		
2.		
3.		
4.		
5.		
6.		
7.		
8.		
9.		
10.		

Whether it was a spark with no fire or it's still burning, list all of your crushes (celebrity or otherwise) and see if you have a type.

HOW LONG IT LASTED	FAVORITE MEMORY

Best Memories with Best Friends

FRIEND
1.
2.
3.
4.
5.
6.
7.
8.
9.
10.

All friends bring a certain levity to your life. Reflect on your nearest and dearest companions (old and new) and recall your favorite memories of them.

MEMORY

My Parents' Stories

"There is no friendship, no love, like that of the parent for the child."

—HENRY WARD BEECHER

What is the earliest memory I have of my parents?

☆

★

What did my parents want to be when they grew up?

☆

★

How would I describe my parents to someone who has never met them?

☆

★

How are my parents similar? How are they different?

☆

★

Who are my parents' closest friends? Describe their friendships.

☆

★

If my parents were on a desert island, what three things would they bring with them and why?

☆

★

What physical traits do I get from my parents? What personality traits?

☆

★

What talents did I inherit from my parents?

☆

★

If my parents could live anywhere, where would they choose and why?

☆

★

How would I describe the parenting style of my parents?

☆

★

Who are my parents' heroes?

☆

★

What were my parents' college experiences like? If they didn't go to college, why didn't they?

☆

★

What would an ideal day look like for my parents?

☆

★

What are some sounds, smells, tastes, and textures that remind me of my parents?

☆

★

How did my parents make holidays festive?

☆

★

What is an activity I used to do with my parents?

☆

★

What types of jobs have my parents had? Which ones did they enjoy the most?

☆

★

Do my parents have any nicknames for me? Tell the story behind each nickname.

☆

★

What extracurriculars did my parents participate in when they were young?

☆

★

What is my parents' sense of humor? What makes them laugh?

☆

★

What are three events that shaped my parents? How did those events change them?

☆

★

List the reasons I am thankful for my parents.

☆

★

Would I be friends with my parents if I grew up with them? Why or why not?

☆

★

When did I feel most comforted by my parents?

☆

★

Things Parents Always Say

"

"

Parents say the darndest things. Write down the stories they tell at every holiday gathering or the quotes they quip as little bits of wisdom. Use one side for each parent or just add quotes as they come to mind.

66

99

Parental Hero Moments

DATE	PARENT	WHAT THEY DID

Use this chart to catalogue some of
your favorite memories of your parents.

HOW IT MADE YOU FEEL	WHAT YOU REMEMBER MOST ABOUT IT

If My Parent Were a(n)...

CAR	
ANIMAL	
PLANET	
PLANT	
SNACK FOOD	
FAST FOOD CHAIN	
VACATION DESTINATION	
CARTOON CHARACTER	
ACTION MOVIE STAR	
BOOK GENRE	
MOTIVATIONAL POSTER	
MAGAZINE	
YOUTUBE CHANNEL	
VIDEO GAME CHARACTER	
TV SHOW	
SUPERHERO	

They Would Be . . .

SEASON	
CAFFEINATED BEVERAGE	
BREAD	
MONTH	
POP STAR	
NATURAL DISASTER	
SHOE	
ROCK STAR	
HOLIDAY	
DAY OF THE WEEK	
MUSICAL	
MAJOR WORLD CITY	
COLOR	
TEMPERATURE	
PROFESSIONAL SPORT	
TIME OF DAY	

How did my parents meet? When did they fall in love?

☆

★

What did my parents want to be when they grew up? Why?

☆

★

How would my parents describe me as a child?

☆

★

What is my favorite memory of each parent?

☆

★

My Grandparents' Stories

"Nobody can do for little children what grandparents do. Grandparents sort of sprinkle stardust over the lives of little children." **—ALEX HALEY**

CHAPTER THREE

What is the earliest memory I have of my grandparents?

☆

☆

★

★

What did my grandparents want to be when they grew up?

☆

☆

★

★

How are my grandparents similar to my parents? How are they different?

☆

☆

★

★

What are my grandparents' most treasured possessions? Why do they love these objects?

☆

☆

★

★

How would I describe my grandparents to someone who has never met them?

☆

☆

★

★

What do my grandparents like to do in their free time?

☆

☆

★

★

What types of jobs have my grandparents had?

☆

☆

★

★

How did my grandparents meet each other?

☆

☆

★

★

What is one of my favorite memories of my grandparents?

☆

☆

★

★

Did my grandparents go to college? If not, why not?

☆

☆

★

★

Do my grandparents have any nicknames for me? Tell the story behind each nickname.

☆

☆

★

★

How would I describe my grandparents' styles? What are their go-to outfits?

☆

☆

★

★

What was my favorite part of visiting my grandparents? Why?

☆

☆

★

★

What are some sounds, smells, tastes, and textures that remind me of my grandparents?

☆

☆

★

★

What are some of the greatest struggles my grandparents have faced?

☆

☆

★

★

What is an activity I used to do with my grandparents?

☆

☆

★

★

Where have my grandparents lived? What details can I see vividly?

☆

☆

★

★

What stories do I remember my grandparents telling about themselves?

☆

☆

★

★

Name five things my grandparents are talented at.

☆

☆

★

★

What do my grandparents wish they would have known when they were my age?

☆

☆

★

★

What are three events that shaped my grandparents? How did those events change them?

☆

☆

★

★

List the reasons I am thankful for my grandparents.

☆

☆

★

★

How have my grandparents made holidays special?

☆

☆

★

★

What accomplishment(s) are my grandparents most proud of?

☆

☆

★

★

Holiday Memories

TYPE OF HOLIDAY	WHERE IT TOOK PLACE	FUNNY MEMORY

Use this chart to describe a favorite holiday with your grandparents. If you're around your grandparents while filling out this chart, it could be fun to get their input as well.

FAVORITE FESTIVE FOOD	HIGHLIGHT OF THE DAY

Things Grandparents Always Say

"

"

Grandparents are from a different time than us, and as such, they have some pretty odd and memorable turns-of-phrase. Write down the stories they tell at every holiday gathering or the quotes they quip as little bits of wisdom. Record as many as you can.

Grand-Hero Moments

DATE	GRANDPARENT	WHAT THEY DID

Use this chart to catalogue some of your memories of your grandparents
when they really inspired you the most.

HOW IT MADE YOU FEEL	WHAT YOU REMEMBER MOST ABOUT IT

My Siblings' Stories

"To the outside world, we all grow old. But not to brothers and sisters. We know each other as we always were... We live outside the touch of time." **—CLARA ORTEGA**

What is the earliest memory I have of my siblings?

What did my siblings want to be when they grew up?

How am I like my siblings? How am I different?

What extracurriculars did my siblings participate in when they were young?

What is the best advice I have ever received from my siblings?

What was the biggest fight I had with my siblings when we were children?

When have I laughed the hardest with my siblings?

What were my siblings like in high school?

Do I see my siblings as friends? Why or why not?

What is my siblings' sense of humor? What makes them laugh?

What lessons have my siblings taught me?

How would I describe my siblings' styles? What are their go-to outfits?

What types of jobs have my siblings had? Which ones have they liked the best?

What do I most admire about my siblings? Why?

If my siblings were on a desert island, what three things would they bring with them and why?

What is an activity I used to do all the time with my siblings?

If I could tell my siblings anything, what would it be? Why?

Who are my siblings' heroes?

How have my siblings changed since they were young? How have they stayed the same?

What can I count on my siblings for?

What are three events that shaped my siblings? How did those events change them?

List the reasons I am thankful for my siblings.

What has been my favorite holiday or vacation with my siblings?

When did I feel most comforted by my siblings?

Best Bonding Moments

RANKING	SIBLING

You've known each other for quite some time and are bound to have some interesting memories that solidified your sibling bond. Rank your best memories with your siblings. You can use siblings and friends that feel like siblings.

BONDING MOMENT

All About My Siblings

NAME:	
GREATEST TRAITS:	
WORST FEARS:	
GO-TO OUTFIT:	
FAVORITE HOBBIES:	
FAVORITE FOOD:	
BEST FRIEND:	
DREAM VACATION:	

NAME:	
GREATEST TRAITS:	
WORST FEARS:	
GO-TO OUTFIT:	
FAVORITE HOBBIES:	
FAVORITE FOOD:	
BEST FRIEND:	
DREAM VACATION:	

Fill in each box for one of your siblings. Get creative with the space you have left if you have less than four siblings, or no siblings at all. You can use siblings and friends that feel like siblings.

NAME:	
GREATEST TRAITS:	
WORST FEARS:	
GO-TO OUTFIT:	
FAVORITE HOBBIES:	
FAVORITE FOOD:	
BEST FRIEND:	
DREAM VACATION:	

NAME:	
GREATEST TRAITS:	
WORST FEARS:	
GO-TO OUTFIT:	
FAVORITE HOBBIES:	
FAVORITE FOOD:	
BEST FRIEND:	
DREAM VACATION:	

Best Things About Having Siblings

NAME	NICKNAMES	BEST THING ABOUT THEM

You probably have a million things to chose from, but fill in the following charts as an homage to what makes your sibling(s) so great. You can use siblings and friends that feel like siblings.

FAVORITE MEMORIES

What is your favorite childhood memory of your siblings?

If there was one lesson my siblings could teach me, what would it be?

What were some of the best things about growing up together?

What is a favorite, recent—in the last 5 years—memory of my siblings?

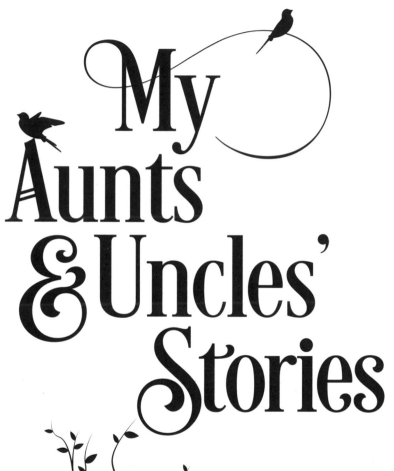

My Aunts & Uncles' Stories

"Only an aunt can give hugs like a mother, keep secrets like a sister, and share love like a friend." **—UNKNOWN**

What is the earliest memory I have of my aunts and uncles?

☆

☆

★

★

How have my aunts and uncles made holidays special?

☆

☆

★

★

When I imagine my aunts and uncles, where do I see them?

☆

☆

★

★

What is one of my favorite childhood memories with my aunts and uncles?

☆

☆

★

★

Which aunt or uncle do I trust the most? Why?

☆

☆

★

★

What jobs have my aunts and uncles held?

☆

☆

★

★

What talents do my aunts and uncles have?

☆

☆

★

★

How has my relationship changed over the years with my aunts and uncles?

☆

☆

★

★

If I had to spend a week with an aunt or uncle, who would it be? Why?

☆

☆

★

★

How were my aunts and uncles as parents?

☆

☆

★

★

Who are my aunts and uncles' heroes?

☆

☆

★

★

What is my aunts and uncles' sense of humor? What makes them laugh?

☆

☆

★

★

What is the best advice I have received from my aunts and uncles?

☆

☆

★

★

What major life lessons have my aunts and uncles taught me?

☆

☆

★

★

How would I describe my aunts and uncles to people who have never met them?

☆

☆

★

★

Do my aunts and uncles have any nicknames for me? Tell the story behind each nickname.

☆

☆

★

★

What extracurriculars did my aunts and uncles participate in their youth?

☆

☆

★

★

What is an activity I used to do with my aunts and uncles?

☆

☆

★

★

If I could tell my aunts and uncles one things, what would it be?

☆

☆

★

★

How would my aunts and uncles describe my parents (their siblings)?

☆

☆

★

★

What would an ideal day look like for my aunts and uncles?

☆

☆

★

★

What do I admire about my aunts and uncles?

☆

☆

★

★

What are three events that shaped my aunts and uncles? How did those events change them?

☆

☆

★

★

List the reasons I am thankful for my aunts and uncles.

☆

☆

★

★

All About My Aunts and Uncles

NAME	NICKNAMES	1-10 AWESOME SCALE

Rate how amazing, funny, engaging, and supportive your aunts and uncles are with these pages. List out your favorite memories and odd nicknames so you'll never forget.

FAVORITE MEMORIES

If My Aunts and Uncles Were a(n)...

	AUNT/UNCLE
ANIMAL	
PLANET	
PLANT	
SNACK FOOD	
FAST FOOD CHAIN	
VACATION DESTINATION	
CARTOON CHARACTER	
ACTION MOVIE STAR	
BOOK GENRE	
MOTIVATIONAL POSTER	
MAGAZINE	
YOUTUBE CHANNEL	
VIDEO GAME CHARACTER	
TV SHOW	
SUPERHERO	

Answer these silly questions about your aunts and uncles.

THEY WOULD BE . . .

Best Things About Having Aunts and Uncles

AUNT/UNCLE	DESCRIBE THEM IN ONE WORD

It's not a competition, but some of your family members have a *je ne c'est quoi* about them that makes them that much more relatable. Fill in the following chart about your aunts and uncles with your favorite parts about them.

BEST THING ABOUT THEM

My Cousins' Stories

"A cousin is a little bit of childhood that can never be lost." **—MARION C. GARRETTY**

What is the earliest memory I have of my cousins?

☆

★

What did my cousins want to be when they grew up?

☆

★

Which cousin was I closest to as a child? Why do I think that is?

☆

★

Which cousin am I closest to as an adult? Why do I think that is?

☆

★

What is a favorite memory I have with my cousins?

☆

★

When have I laughed the hardest with my cousins?

☆

★

What were my cousins like as children? How have they changed?

☆

★

What is your favorite cousin's sense of humor? What makes them laugh?

☆

★

When I picture my cousins, where are they?

☆

★

How are my cousins' immediate families different from my own?

☆

★

What is one favorite holiday or vacation memory of my cousins?

☆

★

If my cousins were on a desert island, what three things would they bring with them? Why?

☆

★

What lessons have my cousins taught me?

☆

★

What is an activity I used to do with my cousins?

☆

★

Do my cousins enjoy their jobs? Why or why not?

☆

★

If I could tell my cousins one thing, what would it be?

☆

★

Who are my cousins' heroes?

☆

★

Which of my cousins do I admire the most? Why?

☆

★

What are three events that shaped my cousins? How did those events change them?

☆

★

List the reasons I am thankful for my cousins.

☆

★

How am I like my cousins? How am I different?

☆

★

When did I feel most comforted by my cousins?

☆

★

What special talents do my cousins have?

☆

★

How would life be different without my cousins?

☆

★

My Closest Cousins

NAME	DESCRIBE IN 3 WORDS

Cousins can be your nearest and dearest friends as soon as you're born. You probably have a slew of different memories of them. While it might be hard to pack so much into so few words, try to distill them down into just three.

FAVORITE MEMORY

Greatest Cousin Adventures

DATE	COUSIN

Vacations, road trips, shenanigans, oh my! Fill out the adventures you've had (or the adventure you want to have) with your cousins in the table below.

ADVENTURE

Hero Moments

DATE	WHAT THEY DID

When we think of heroes, a lot of the time we think of people who are significantly older than us. Use this space to write down your cousins' most memorable displays of bravery that inspired you to be a better version of yourself.

HOW IT MADE YOU FEEL	WHAT YOU REMEMBER MOST ABOUT IT

What is the funniest childhood memory I have of my cousins?

☆

★

If there was one lesson my cousins could teach me, what would it be?

☆

★

What were some of the best things about growing up together?

☆

★

What is a favorite, recent—in the last 5 years—memory of my cousins?

☆

★

Inspiring | Educating | Creating | Entertaining

Brimming with creative inspiration, how-to projects, and useful information to enrich your everyday life, Quarto Knows is a favorite destination for those pursuing their interests and passions. Visit our site and dig deeper with our books into your area of interest: Quarto Creates, Quarto Cooks, Quarto Homes, Quarto Lives, Quarto Drives, Quarto Explores, Quarto Gifts, or Quarto Kids.

© 2021 Quarto Publishing Group USA Inc.

First published in 2021 by Chartwell Books,
an imprint of The Quarto Group,
142 West 36th Street, 4th Floor,
New York, NY 10018 USA
T (212) 779-4972 · F (212) 779-6058
www.QuartoKnows.com

Chartwell Books titles are also available at discount for retail, wholesale, promotional, and bulk purchase. For details, contact the Special Sales Manager by email at specialsales@quarto.com or by mail at The Quarto Group, Attn: Special Sales Manager, 100 Cummings Center Suite 265D, Beverly, MA 01915, USA.

10 9 8 7 6 5 4 3 2 1

ISBN: 978-0-7858-3955-2

Publisher: Rage Kindelsperger
Creative Director: Laura Drew
Managing Editor: Cara Donaldson
Project Editor: Leeann Moreau
Cover and Interior Design: Beth Middleworth

Printed in China

This book provides general information. It should not be relied upon as recommending or promoting any specific diagnosis or method of treatment for a particular condition, and it is not intended as a substitute for medical advice or for direct diagnosis and treatment of a medical condition by a qualified physician. Readers who have questions about a particular condition, possible treatments for that condition, or possible reactions from the condition or its treatment should consult a physician or other qualified healthcare professional.